U.S. Army, War Departement

Manual of calisthenic exercises

U.S. Army, War Departement

Manual of calisthenic exercises

ISBN/EAN: 9783742833105

Manufactured in Europe, USA, Canada, Australia, Japa

Cover: Foto ©Stingray / pixelio.de

Manufactured and distributed by brebook publishing software
(www.brebook.com)

U.S. Army, War Departement

Manual of calisthenic exercises

This volume, prepared under the supervision of

and published by the War Department, is the property of the United States and by direction of the Secretary of War is deposited with *Company "C" 13th Infantry* for official use.

Section 74 of the act of Congress approved January 12, 1895, provides as follows:

"Government publications furnished to judicial and executive officers of the United States for their official use shall not become the property of these officers, but on the expiration of their official term shall be by them delivered to their successors in office, and all Government publications delivered to designated depositories or other libraries shall be for public use without charge."

MANUAL

OF

CALISTHENIC EXERCISES.

BY AUTHORITY OF

THE WAR DEPARTMENT.

WASHINGTON:
GOVERNMENT PRINTING OFFICE.
1892.

WAR DEPARTMENT,

Washington, D. C., December 4, 1891.

This Manual of Calisthenic Exercise, prepared by Mr. Herman J. Koehler, master of the sword at the Military Academy, is published for the information of all concerned. Any calisthenic instruction of enlisted men that may be carried on should be in accordance with the provisions of this system.

REDFIELD PROCTOR,
Secretary of War.

III

PREFACE.

The system of calisthenic exercises contained in this work is substantially the method devised by Mr. Herman J. Koehler, Swordmaster at the United States Military Academy, and used in the instruction of cadets since the introduction of the present system of physical training. Some months since, the Superintendent of the Academy, Col. John M. Wilson, Corps of Engineers, perceiving the "wonderful effect upon the carriage and bearing of the younger cadets of the calisthenic exercises as developed by Mr. Koehler," suggested to him the propriety of preparing and publishing his system for the use of the Army and Militia of the United States, and to this end Col. Wilson had photographs taken, showing by figures the positions described in the text. After preparing his manuscript, Mr. Koehler very courteously tendered it to the Adjutant-General of the Army for the use of the troops, and the same having been reviewed by a board of officers, in order that the system might be adapted to the new drill regulations, the honorable the Secretary of War directed that all calisthenic instruction for enlisted men should be in accordance with Mr. Koehler's system.

The system herein prescribed includes merely the fundamental exercises, combinations having been purposely avoided, but they will suggest themselves in infinite variety in cases where time and occasion permit. It is intended to be preliminary to all other forms of gymnastics, and supplementary to the setting up exercises prescribed by the drill regulations of the several arms of the service. They should be thoroughly learned before the squad is advanced to the use of special gymnastic apparatus, as a preparation for such more violent

exercises.   The plates which illustrate the work were
made from photographs taken at West Point, the de-
tailed motions of many of the calisthenic exercises having
been illustrated by Lieut. George H. Cameron, Seventh
Cavalry.   In its work the board of officers was ably
assisted by Lieut. Peter E. Traub, First Cavalry.

CONTENTS.

CALISTHENIC EXERCISES.

ADVICE TO INSTRUCTORS.

Only those who are masters of this system of calisthenics should undertake to act as instructors.

The drill should be made as attractive as possible, and this can be best accomplished by employing the mind as well as the body. The movements should be as varied as possible, thus offering the men constantly something new to make them keep their minds on their work. A movement many times repeated presents no attraction; and is executed in a purely mechanical manner, which should always be discountenanced.

The exercises should be vigorously executed; and to properly discipline the muscles, which is one of the many valuable features of this method, the greatest accuracy and precision should at all times be insisted on.

Short and frequent drills should be given in preference to long ones, which are liable to exhaust all concerned, and exhaustion means injury. All movements should be carefully explained, and, if necessary, illustrated by the instructor.

The lesson should begin with the less violent exercises, gradually working up to those that are more so, then gradually working back to the simpler ones, so that the men at the close of the drill will be in as nearly a normal condition as possible.

When one portion of the body is being exercised, care should be taken that the other parts remain quiet as far as the conformation of the body will allow. The men must learn to exercise any one portion of the body by itself.

The movements of an exercise are executed by command; the portion of the command corresponding to

1

16200——1

that movement which is to be *accented,* that is, executed with most vigor, should be *emphasized.*

Judgment must be used in giving commands, for rarely is the cadence of two exercises alike, and commands should indicate not only the cadence of the exercise, but also the rapidity of execution; for instance:

All or nearly all of the movements in the arm exercises are short and quick; hence the commands should be given in a brief tone, following one another in quick succession.

Again, the movements in the leg and foot exercises can not be executed as quickly as in the arm exercises, therefore, the commands should be slightly drawn out and should follow one another more slowly.

Finally, in the trunk exercises, owing to the deliberateness of execution, the commands should be considerably drawn out and should follow one another in slow succession.

Instructors should never lose sight of the fact that they are dealing with and understand the human body; they should allow frequent rests, and take into consideration the condition of the men and their surroundings, the time of day, etc.: they should at all times encourage and urge the men to improve in their work; by so doing, they will accomplish great good; by neglecting these facts, they may work irreparable harm.

DRESS.

Flannel is the best material to wear next the body in gymnastic exercises, as it absorbs the perspiration, protects the body against drafts, and, in a mild manner, excites the skin. The shirt should be made like an ordinary tourist's shirt, with collar cut low. The trousers should be loose about the legs and held in position by an elastic belt. A tight belt or tight clothing of any kind is positively injurious. Shoes when worn indoors should be made of a light, pliable material, such as canvas or leather, with a light leather heelless sole. For outdoor drills a regulation tennis shoe is best.

HYGIENE.

Everything in connection with physical culture should be such that the men look forward to calisthenics and gymnastics with pleasure, not with dread, for the mind exerts more influence over the human body than all the gymnastic paraphernalia that was ever invented.

Exercise should be carried on as much as possible in the open air; at all times in pure, dry air.

Only those men whom the post surgeon declares to be physically qualified and sure to be benefited thereby should be put through a course of physical training. The old, the rheumatic, and those who require physical exercise as a therapeutic agent have no business in a gymnasium.

Never exercise the body to the point of exhaustion. If you pant, feel faint or tired, or experience pain, stop at once, for it is nature's way of saying *"too much."*

By constant practice learn to breathe slowly through the nose during all exercise, especially running.

"A fundamental condition of exercise is unimpeded respiration." Proper breathing should always be insisted upon; "holding the breath" or breathing only when it can no longer be held is as injurious as light clothing. Every exercise should be accompanied by an unimpeded and if possible by an uninterrupted act of respiration, the inspiration and expiration of which depend to a great extent upon the nature of the exercise. Inhalation should always accompany that part of our exercise which tends to elevate and distend the thorax— as raising arms over head latterly, for instance; while that part of an exercise which exerts a pressure against the walls of the chest should be accompanied by exhalation, and lowering arms latterly from shoulders or overhead, for example.

If after exercising the breathing becomes labored and distressful, it is an unmistakable sign that the work has been excessive. Such excessiveness is not infrequently the cause of serious injury to the heart or lungs, or to both. In cases where exercise produces palpitation, labored respiration, etc., it is advisable to recommend absolute rest, or to order the execution of such exercises as will relieve the oppressed and overtaxed organ. Leg exercises slowly extended will afford great relief. By drawing the blood from the upper to the lower extremities they equalize the circulation, thereby lessening the heart's action and quieting the respiration. For such exercises see Leg Exercises.

Never exercise immediately after a meal; digestion is more important at this time than extraneous exercise.

Never eat or drink immediately after exercise; allow the body to recover its normal condition first, and the most beneficial results will follow.

If necessary, pure water, not too cold, may be taken in small quantities, but the exercise should be continued, especially if in a state of perspiration.

Never, if at all possible, allow the underclothing to dry on the body.

Muscular action produces an unusual amount of bodily heat; this should be lost gradually, otherwise the body will be chilled; hence, after exercise, *never* take off clothing, but, on the contrary, wear some wrap in addition. In like manner, be well wrapped on leaving the gymnasium.

Cold baths, especially when the body is heated, as is the case after exercising violently, should be discouraged. In individual instances such baths may appear apparently beneficial, or at least not injurious; in the majority of cases, however, they can not be used with impunity. Tepid baths are recommended. When impossible to bathe, the flannels worn while exercising should be stripped off, the body sponged with tepid water, and then rubbed thoroughly with coarse towels. After such a sponge bath the body should be clothed in clean, warm clothing.

COMMANDS.

There are two kinds of commands:
The *preparatory* indicates the movement to be executed.
The command of *execution* causes the execution.

In the command: 1. *Arms forward*, 2. RAISE, the words *arms forward* constitute the preparatory command, and *raise,* the command of execution. Preparatory commands are printed in *italics*, and those of execution in CAPITALS.

The tone of command is animated, distinct, and of a loudness proportioned to the number of men under instruction. Each preparatory command is pronounced in an ascending tone of voice, but in such a manner that the command of execution, always in a firm and brief tone, may be more energetic and elevated.

THE POSITION OF ATTENTION.

This is the position that an unarmed, dismounted soldier assumes when in ranks. During the calisthenic exercises, it is assumed whenever the command *attention,* or *halt,* is given by the instructor.

Having allowed his men to rest, the instructor commands: 1. *Squad,* 2. ATTENTION.

The words class, section, or company may be substituted for the word squad.

At *attention,* the men will quickly assume and retain the following position:

Heels on same line and as near each other as the conformation of the man permits.

Feet turned out equally and forming with each other an angle of about 60°.

Knees straight, and, if possible, without stiffness, closed.

The body erect on the hips, inclining a little forward.

Shoulders well back and square, thus throwing out and slightly raising the chest.

Arms and hands hanging naturally; elbows near the body; backs of hands turned outward; little fingers opposite the seams of the trousers.

Head erect and square to the front; chin slightly drawn in, without constraint; eyes straight to the front.

FORMATION.

The men form in a single rank, tallest man on the right.

The instructor commands: 1. *Count*, 2. **FOURS**.

Beginning on the right, the men count one, two, three, four, and so on, to the left.

The instructor then commands : 1. *Fours right* (or *left*), 2. **MARCH**, 3. *Squad*, 4. **HALT**.

At the command *march*, each set of fours wheels 90° to the right on a fixed pivot, halting at *halt*.

To take intervals, he then commands : 1. *To the right* (or *left*) *take intervals*, 2. **MARCH**.

At the command *march*, the man on the left of each four stands fast; the other men face to the right and step off, each man halting faced to the front, when he has the proper interval of two paces.

To prove intervals, he then commands : 1. *Prove*, 2. **INTERVALS**.

At the command *intervals*, the men raise their arms laterally to the horizontal position, giving way in case they touch their neighbors' hands; they then resume the attention.

To rest the men, the instructor commands : **FALL OUT**, or **REST**, or **AT EASE**.

At the command *fall out*, the men may leave the ranks, but will remain in the immediate vicinity ; at the command *fall in*, they resume their former places.

At the command *rest*, the men keep one heel in place, but are not required to preserve silence or immobility.

At the command *at ease,* the men keep one heel in place and preserve silence, but not immobility.

To resume the attention: 1. *Squad,* 2. **ATTENTION.**

To assemble, the instructor commands: 1. *To the right* (or *left*) *assemble,* 2. **MARCH.**

At the command *march,* the man on the right of each four stands fast, the other men close to their proper places.

To form line to the left or right: 1. *Fours left* (or *right*), 2. **MARCH,** 3. *Squad,* 4. **HALT.**

Being in line at a halt, to dismiss the squad, the instructor commands: **DISMISSED.**

SPECIAL TRAINING.

In addition to the regular squad or class work, instructors should, when they notice a physical defect in any man, recommend some exercise which will tend to correct it.

The most common physical defects and corresponding corrective exercises are noted here.

Drooping Head.

Exercise the muscles of the neck by bending, turning, and circling the head.

Round and Stooped Shoulders.

Swing arms sideward and forward.
Circle arms backward.
Move shoulders backward and forward.
Circle shoulders backward.

Weak Back.

Bend trunk forward and obliquely forward.

Weak Abdomen.

Bend trunk backward and obliquely backward; circle trunk.

Swing arms upward, forcing them as far to the rear as possible when overhead.

Bend trunk backward and raise arms overhead at the same time.

To Increase Depth and Width of Chest.

Recommend:

Shoulder exercises.

Arm swings and arm circles.

Raising arms overhead laterally, and crossing them as far as possible in that position.

EXERCISES.

STARTING POSITIONS.

In nearly all the arm exercises it is necessary to hold the arms in some fixed position from which the exercise can be most advantageously executed, and to which position the arms are again returned upon completing the exercise. These positions are termed *starting positions;* and, though it may not be absolutely neccessary to assume one of them before or during the exercising of any other portion of the body, it is advisable to do so, since they give to the exercise a finished and graceful appearance.

In the following eleven positions, at the command *down,* resume the attention. Each exercise may be continued by repeating the commands of execution, such as *raise, down.*

Intervals having been taken and attention assumed, the instructor commands:

1. 1. *Arms forward,* 2. **RAISE,** 3. **DOWN.** Fig. 1.

Fig. 1.

At the command *raise,* raise the arms to the front smartly, extended to their full length, till the hands are in front of and at the height of the shoulders, palms down, fingers extended and joined, thumbs under forefingers.

Fig. 2.

2. 1. *Arms sideward,* 2. RAISE, 3. DOWN. Fig. 2.

At the command *raise,* raise the arms laterally until horizontal; palms down, fingers as in 1.

The arms are brought down smartly, but stopped just before reaching the body.

3. 1. *Arms upward,* 2. RAISE, 3. DOWN. Fig. 3.

At the command *raise,* raise the arms from the sides, extended to their full length, with the forward movement, until vertical overhead. Back of the hand turned outward; fingers as in 1.

Fig. 3.

This position may also be assumed by raising the arms laterally until vertical. The instructor cautions which way he desires it done.

4. 1. *Arms forward,* 2. C R O S S, 3. DOWN. Fig. 4.

At the command *cross,* the arms are folded over the chest; thumbs under and fingers closed over the biceps.

Fig. 4.

5. 1. *Arms backward,* 2. CROSS, 3. DOWN. Fig. 5.

At the command *cross,* the arms are folded across the back; hands grasping forearms.

Fig. 5.

6. 1. *Arms to thrust,* 2. RAISE, 3. DOWN. Fig. 6.

Fig. 6.

At the command *raise,* raise the forearms to the front

until horizontal, elbow forced back, upper arms against the chest, hands tightly closed, backs down.

7. 1. *Hands on hips*, 2. **PLACE**, 3. **DOWN**. Fig. 7.

At the command *place*, place the hands on the hips, so that the thumbs meet in the small of the back, fingers extended and joined, tips forward; elbows pressed back.

8. 1. *Hands on shoulders*, 2. **PLACE**, 3. **DOWN**. Fig. 8.

At the command *place*, raise the forearms to the vertical position, palms inward, without moving the upper arms; then raise the elbows upward and outward until the upper arms are horizontal, at the same time bending the wrist and allowing the finger tips to rest lightly on the shoulders.

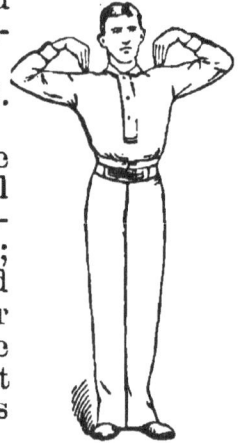

Fig. 7.

9. 1. *Hands forward*, 2. **CLASP**, 3. **DOWN**. Fig. 9.

At the command *clasp*, clasp the hands in front of the center of the body, left hand uppermost, left thumb clasped by right hand.

10. 1. *Hands backward*, 2. **CLASP**, 2. **DOWN**.

Same as in 9, but behind the body.

11. 1. *Fingers in rear of head*, 2. **LACE**, 3. **DOWN**. Fig. 10.

At the command *lace*, raise the arms and forearms as described in 8, and lace the fingers behind the lower portion of head, elbows well up and pressed well back.

Fig. 9.

These positions should be prac-

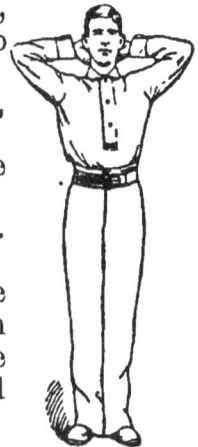

Fig. 8.

Fig. 10.

ticed frequently, and, instead of recovering the position of attention after each exercise, the instructor may change directly from one to another, by giving the proper commands, instead of commanding *down*.

For instance: To change from 8 to 9 (having commanded, 1. *Hands on Shoulders*, 2. PLACE), he commands: 1. *Hands forward*, 2. CLASP.

These changes should, however, be made only after the positions are thoroughly understood and correctly assumed.

ARM.

I. RAISING.

1. Raise arm, or arms, forward. (See Fig. 1.)
2. Raise arm, or arms, sideward.   (See Fig. 2.)
3. Raise arm, or arms, upward (forward motion). (See Fig. 3.)
4. Raise arm, or arms, upward (lateral motion).
5. Raise arm, or arms, backward.
6. Raise arm, or arms, forward (obliquely downward).
7. Raise arm, or arms, forward (obliquely upward). Fig. 11.
8. Raise arm, or arms, sideward (obliquely downward). Fig. 12.
9. Raise arm, or arms, sideward (obliquely upward).
10. Raise arm, or arms, obliquely downward. Fig. 13.

Fig. 11.

Fig. 12.

11. Raise arm, or arms, obliquely forward.
12. Raise arm, or arms, obliquely upward.
13. Raise arm, or arms, obliquely backward.

Fig. 13.

Command: 1. *Arms forward,* 2. **RAISE,** 3. **DOWN.**

At the command *raise,* in this series, the arms are raised to the specified position with life. At *down,* they are lowered to sides.

The exercise may be continued by repeating *raise, down.* Whenever the arms are held in the horizontal position, or below the horizontal, the backs are turned up; in all positions above the horizontal, they are turned outward.

II. SWINGING.

1. Swing arm, or arms, downward and forward. Fig. 14*a.*

2. Swing arm, or arms, sideward and forward. Fig. 14*b.*

3. Swing arm, or arms, upward and forward.

4. Swing arm, or arms, upward and downward, forward motion.

5. Swing arm, or arms, upward and downward, lateral motion.

Command: 1. *Arms downward and forward ;* 2. **SWING.**

Continue by repeating *One, two.*

Exercises 1, 2, 3 are executed from the position *arms forward* ; 4, 5, from *arms upward.*

The arms remain fully extended while being swung. In the down-

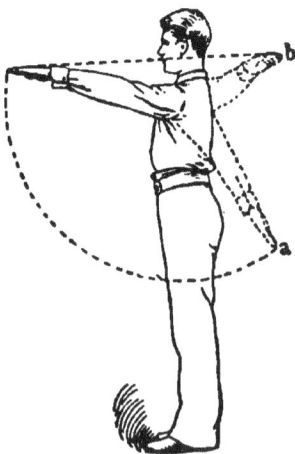

Fig. 14.

ward swing, the arms are forced back as far as possible, remaining parallel to the sides of the body; in the sideward or horizontal swing, they are also forced well back; in the upward swing care should be taken to prevent the elbows being bent.

III. THRUSTING.

1. Thrust arm, or arms, forward.
2. Thrust arm, or arms, sideward.
3. Thrust arm, or arms, upward.
4. Thrust arm, or arms, downward.
5. Thrust arm, or arms, in the various oblique directions.

Command: 1. *Arms forward,* 2. **THRUST**, 3. **BACK**.
Continue by repeating *Thrust, Back.*

These exercises are executed from the position *arms to thrust.* The arms are forcibly extended in the direction indicated. In thrusting forward and sideward, the arms are turned so that the knuckles are up; in the upward, so that they are out; in the downward, so that they are forward. At the command *back,* the position of *arms to thrust* is resumed.

IV. EXTENDING.

1. Extend arm, or arms, forward.
2. Extend arm, or arms, sideward.
3. Extend arm, or arms, upward.
4. Extend arm, or arms, downward.
5. Extend arm, or arms, in the various oblique directions.

Command: 1. *Arms sideward,* 2. **EXTEND**, 3. **BACK**.

These exercises are usually executed from the position of *hands on shoulders or hips.* At the command *extend,* the first thing is to turn the hand in such a manner that the finger tips point in the direction in which the arms are to be extended. In the forward and sideward extension, the knuckles are turned up; in the upward extension, they are turned out; and in the downward, forward.

Continue the exercise by repeating *extend, back.*

V. STRIKING.

1. Strike right, or left, arm sideward. Fig. 15.
2. Strike both arms sideward.
3. Strike right, or left, arm forward.
4. Strike both arms forward.

Fig. 15.

Command: 1. *Arms sideward,* 2. **STRIKE**, 3. **BACK**.

In striking, the hand is closed tightly; the knuckles are turned down.   Both the striking movement and return to position indicated by instructor should be executed with life.

Continue by repeating *strike, back.*

VI. CIRCLING.

1. Circle arm, or arms, forward.   Fig. 16*a*.
2. Circle arm, or arms, backward.   Fig. 16*b*.

3. Circle arm, or arms, inward. Fig. 17*a*.
4. Circle arm, or arms, outward. Fig. 17*b*.

5. Circle right arm backward and left arm forward.

6. Circle left arm backward and right arm forward.

Command: 1. *Arms forward,* 2. **CIRCLE.**

Execute from position of *arms upward.*

At command *circle,* swing the arms around in as large a circle as possible, keeping them fully extended and the hands tightly closed.

Continue by repeating *One, two.*

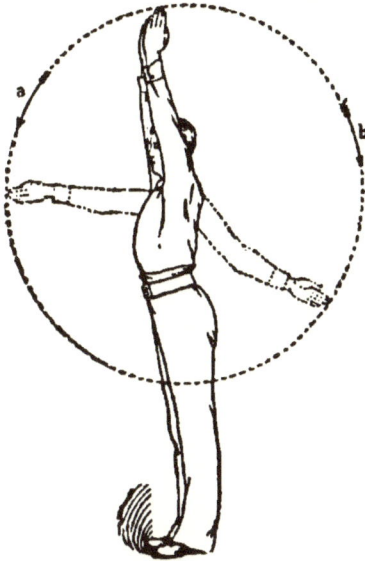

Fig. 16.

VII. FUNNELING.

1. Funnel arm, or arms, forward. Fig. 18.

2. Funnel arm, or arms, backward.

3. Funnel right arm forward and left backward.

4. Funnel left arm forward and right backward.

Command: 1. *Arms forward,* 2. **FUNNEL.**

Continue by repeating *One, two.*

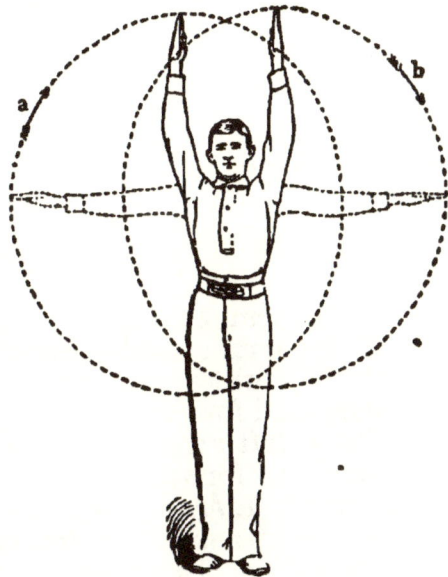

Fig. 17.

16200——2

Execute 1, 2, 3, 4, from *arms sideward.* From *arms forward*, the funneling would be inward or outward; so that the complete command, from attention, would be: 1. *Arms forward*, 2. **RAISE**, 3. *Arms inward*, 4. **FUNNEL**, 5. etc., **FUNNEL, HALT.**

Fig. 18.

This command is introduced here, to indicate how all are to be given. The diameter of circle described by the hand is about 12 inches.

VIII. TWISTING.

1. Twist arm, or arms, forward and backward.
2. Twist arm, or arms, backward and forward.
3. Twist right arm forward and backward, left arm backward and forward.
4. Twist left arm forward and backward, right arm backward and forward.
Command: 1. *Arms forward and backward*, 2. **TWIST.**
Continue by repeating *One, two.*
Execute from *arms sideward.* Twist the arms forward with a rotary motion, until the knuckles are turned for-

ward; then twist them backward, till the knuckles are turned down. The whole arm, from the shoulder joint, should be rotated upon an axis within, passing from shoulder to wrist.

WRIST AND FINGER.

I. BENDING.

1. Bend wrists downward. Fig. 19*a*.
2. Bend wrists upward. Fig. 19*b*.
3. Bend wrists backward.
4. Bend fingers downward.
5. Bend fingers upward.
6. Bend wrists downward and upward.
7. Bend fingers downward and upward.

Command: 1. *Wrists downward,* 2. **BEND,** 3. **BACK.**

Exercises 1 to 7 are continued by repeating *One, two.*

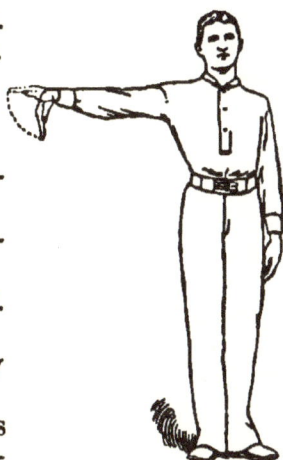

Fig. 19 a.

While the wrists or fingers are being exercised, the arms should remain fully extended.

Usually executed from *arms upward, forward,* or *sideward.*

II. CIRCLING, SPREADING, AND CLOSING.

1. Circle wrists forward.
2. Circle wrists backward.
3. Spread and close fingers.
4. Close and open hands.

Command: 1. *Hands,* 2. **CLOSE,** 3. **OPEN.**

Fig. 19 b.

Continue by repeating *close, open.*
1. *Wrists,* 2. *Forward*, 3. CIRCLE.
Continue by repeating *circle.*
1. *Fingers,* 2. SPREAD, 3. CLOSE.
Continue by repeating *spread, close.*

In 1, 2, the hands are swung around in a circle as quickly as possible, without bending the elbows. In spreading the fingers, they should be separated as far as possible and closed with life.

In 4 the hand should be closed tightly and opened with life.

NECK.

I. TURNING.

1. Turn head to the right.   Fig. 20.

Fig. 20.

2. Turn head to the left.
3. Turn head to the right and left.
Command: 1. *Head right,* 2. TURN, 3. BACK.

In 3, continue by repeating *One, two.*
Turn the head in the direction indicated until the chin is directly over the shoulder.

II. BENDING.

1. Bend head forward.
2. Bend head backward. Fig. 21.
3. Bend head sideward, right.
4. Bend head sideward, left. Fig. 22.
5. Bend head forward and backward.
6. Bend head sideward, right and left.

Command: 1. *Head forward,* 2. **BEND,** 3. **BACK.**

Continue, in 5, 6, by repeating *One, two.*

Fig. 21.
Bend the head forward till the
Fig. 22.

·chin rests on the chest: bend backward and sideward as far as possible.

III. CIRCLING.

1. Circle head to right.
2. Circle head to left.
Command: 1. *Head right,* 2. **CIRCLE.**
Continue by repeating *One, two.*
The head is first bent forward; it is then moved to the right, then backward, then to the left; it is bent forward again, and finally raised.

IV. SWINGING.

1. Swing head forward and backward.
2. Swing head to the right and left.
Command: 1. *Head forward and backward,* 2. **SWING.**
Continue by repeating *swing.*

These exercises are similar to the bendings, only they are executed quicker. If desired to execute these or any

other exercises without pausing, the command *continue the exercise* should be given after the above or other commands, as explained under *commands.*

During the execution of the neck exercises the hands are placed preferably on the hips.

SHOULDER.

I. RAISING.

1. Raise right shoulder. Fig. 23.
2. Raise left shoulder.
3. Raise both shoulders. Fig. 24.
4. Raise right and left shoulders alternately.
Command: 1 *Right shoulder*, 2. RAISE, 3. DOWN.
In 4, continue by repeating *One, two.*

Fig. 23.

Fig. 24.

Raise the shoulders as high as possible and lower with force.

II. MOVING.

1. Move right shoulder forward.
2. Move left shoulder forward.
3. Move left shoulder backward.
4. Move right shoulder backward.
5. Move both shoulders backward. Fig. 26.
6. Move both shoulders forward. Fig. 25.
7. Move both shoulders forward and backward.
Command: 1. *Shoulders forward*, 2. MOVE, 3. BACK.
In 7, continue by repeating *One, two.*

Fig. 25.

Fig. 26.

The shoulders should be moved forward and backward with life and as far as possible.

III. CIRCLING.

1. Circle right, or left, shoulder forward.
2. Circle right, or left, shoulder backward.
3. Circle both shoulders forward.
4. Circle both shoulders backward.
5. Circle right shoulder forward and left backward.
6. Circle left shoulder forward and right backward.
Command: 1. *Shoulders forward,* 2. **CIRCLE.**
Continue by repeating *One, two.*
In the forward circle the shoulders are first moved forward, then raised, then forced back, and finally lowered.

The position of *arms to thrust* should be assumed during the shoulder exercises.

TRUNK.

I. BENDING.

1. Bend trunk forward, quarter bend.   Fig. 27.
2. Bend trunk forward, half bend.   Fig. 28.
   3. Bend trunk forward, full bend. Fig. 29.

Fig. 27.   Fig. 28.   Fig. 29.

4. Bend trunk backward. Fig. 30.

5. Bend trunk sideward, right.

6. Bend trunk sideward, left. Fig. 31.

7. Bend trunk obliquely forward, right. Fig. 32.

8. Bend trunk obliquely forward, left.

9. Bend trunk obliquely backward, right.

10. Bend trunk obliquely backward, left. Fig. 33.

11. Bend trunk forward and backward.

12. Bend trunk sideward, right and left.

Fig. 30.

13. Bend trunk obliquely forward, right, and obliquely backward, left.

14. Bend trunk obliquely forward, left, and obliquely backward, right.

Command: 1. *Trunk sideward,* 2. *Right,* 3. BEND, 4. BACK,

At command *bend,* bend the trunk to the right without twisting it, or bending the knees, or raising the heels. The head, individually, does not move. All of the trunk exercises are executed slowly. In 11, 12, 13, 14, continue by repeating *Qne, two,*

Fig. 31.

II. TURNING.

1. Turn trunk to the right.

2. Turn trunk to the left.

3. Turn trunk to the right and left.

Command: 1. *Trunk right,* 2. TURN, 3. BACK. Fig. 34.

Fig. 32.

Fig. 33.

Turn the trunk on the hips as far as possible, keeping knees straight and feet on the ground.

Fig. 34.

Continue by repeating *One, two.*

III. SWAYING.

1. Sway trunk forward and backward.
2. Sway trunk sideward, right and left.
3. Sway trunk obliquely forward, right, and backward, left.
4. Sway trunk obliquely forward, left, and backward, right.
Command: 1. *Trunk forward and backward,* 2. **SWAY.**
Continue by repeating *One, two.*
These exercises are similar to the *bendings;* the body is moved gently forward and backward, or from side to side; no pause is made, nor is the body bent as much as in the *bendings.*

IV. CIRCLING.

1. Circle trunk to the right.
2. Circle trunk to the left.

Command: 1. *Trunk right,* 2. CIRCLE.

Continue by repeating *One, two.*

In circling, the trunk is bent, first forward, then sideward, next backward, then to the left, forward again, and finally raised.

During the trunk exercises, the arms and hands may assume a number of different positions, preferably, however, *hands on hips.*

LEG.

I. RAISING.

Fig. 35.   Fig. 36.   Fig. 37.

1. Raise right, or left, leg forward, ankle high. Fig, 35.

2. Raise right, or left, leg forward, knee high.

3. Raise right, or left, leg forward, waist high.

4. Raise right, or left, leg backward. Fig. 36.

5. Raise right leg sideward. Fig.37.

6. Raise left leg sideward.

7. Raise right leg obliquely forward right, ankle, knee, or waist high.

8. Raise left leg obliquely forward left, ankle, knee, or waist high.

9. Raise right leg obliquely forward left, ankle, knee, or waist high.

10. Raise left leg obliquely forward, right, ankle, knee, or waist high.

11. Raise right leg obliquely backward, right.

12. Raise left leg obliquely backward, left.

13. Raise right leg obliquely backward, left.

14. Raise left leg obliquely backward, right.

15. Raise right knee forward.   Fig. 38.

Fig. 38.   Fig. 39.   Fig. 40.

16. Raise left knee forward.

17. Raise right knee sideward.   Fig. 39.

18. Raise left knee sideward.

19. Raise right heel backward.

20. Raise left heel backward.   Fig. 40.

Command: 1. *Right leg forward,* 2. *Ankle high,* 3. **RAISE,** 4. **DOWN.**

Exercises 1–14, inclusive, are executed with the knee fully extended, toes depressed.   In raising the knee waist high, the lower leg should be at right angles to the thigh, toes depressed.   When the heels are raised, the knees should not be separated.

II. BENDING.

1. Bend knees, quarter bend. Fig. 41.

Fig. 41.

2. Bend knees, half bend. Fig. 42.

F

3. Bend knees, full bend. Fig. 43.

Command: 1. *Knees quarter,* 2. **BEND,** 3. **BACK.**

Continue by repeating *bend, back.*

In the quarter bend, the foot remains squarely on the floor; in the half bend, the heels are slightly raised; in the full bend, the entire weight of the body rests on the balls of the feet. The heels should be continually in contact, the knees being separated as much as possible. Head and trunk erect.

Fig. 43.

III. SWINGING.

1. Swing right leg forward.
2. Swing left leg forward.
3. Swing right or left leg backward.
4. Swing right or left leg sideward.
5. Swing right leg obliquely forward, right or left.
6. Swing left leg obliquely forward, left or right.
7. Swing right leg obliquely backward, right or left.
8. Swing left leg obliquely backward, left or right.
9. Swing right leg forward and backward.
10. Swing left leg forward and backward.
11. Swing right leg obliquely forward, left, and obliquely backward, right.
12. Swing right leg obliquely forward, right, and obliquely backward, left.
13. Swing left leg obliquely forward, right, and obliquely backward, left.
14. Swing left leg obliquely forward, left, and obliquely backward, right.
15. Circle, swing right leg forward.
16. Circle, swing left leg forward.
17. Circle, swing left leg backward.
18. Circle, swing right leg backward.

Command : 1. *Left leg forward,* 2. SWING.

Continue by repeating *One, two.*

The swinging movement is a short and quick one, the leg, knee fully extended, being swung in the direction indicated and at once returned to the starting position. The body remains erect, the knee of the leg sustaining its weight being rigidly extended.

In exercises 1 to 8, inclusive, the height of swing, whether ankle, knee, waist, shoulder, or head, should be. indicated.

IV. TWISTING.

1. Twist legs outward.   Fig. 44.

2. Twist legs inward.   Fig. 45.

Command: 1. *Legs outward,* 2. TWIST, 3. BACK.

Fig. 44

Fig. 45.

In 1, the lower extremities (hip downward), turning on the heels, are rotated outwards as far as possible.   In 2, they rotate inwards, turning on the balls of the feet till the toe ends of the feet point toward each other.   Body erect, knees straight.   Continue by repeating, *Front, back.*

V. STEPPING.

1. Step forward, right, or left.   Fig. 46.
2. Step sideward, right, or left.
3. Step backward, right, or left.
4. Cross step forward, right, or left.   Fig. 47.
5. Cross step backward, right, or left.

Command: 1. *Right leg forward,* 2. STEP, 3. BACK.

Move the leg, knee extended, toes depressed, in the direction indicated, about twice the length of the foot; ball of the foot on the ground, heel raised.   The other leg remains in position and supports the weight of the body, which remains erect. Recover position of attention smartly at *back.*   Continue by repeating, *Step, back.*

Fig. 46.

Fig. 47.

VI. STRIDING.

1. Stride forward, right, or left.
2. Stride sideward, right, or left.
3. Stride obliquely forward, right, or left.
4. Stride obliquely backward, right, or left.

Command: 1. *Right leg forward,* 2. STRIDE, 3. BACK.

These exercises are similar to the *Stepping* except that the whole foot is planted, the body being supported equally by both legs.   Continue by repeating, *Stride, back.*

In this whole series of leg exercises the arms and hands may be held in any one of the *Starting positions.*

LOWER LEG.

SWINGING, RAISING, CIRCLING.

Preparatory to executing these exercises the instruc-

tor commands: 1. *Right* (or *left*) *lower leg,* 2. EXERCISE.

At the command *Exercise,* raise the knee of the designated leg forward until the thigh is horizontal and lower leg vertical; hands grasping thighs, fingers laced underneath.

1. Swing right, or left, lower leg forward. Fig. 48.

2. Swing right, or left, lower leg backward. Fig. 49.

3. Swing right, or left, lower leg sideward, right or left.

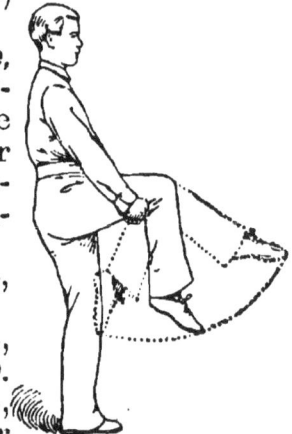

Fig. 48.

Fig. 49.

4. Swing right, or left, lower leg forward and backward. Fig. 49.

5. Swing right, or left, lower leg sideward, right and left. Fig. 50.

6. Raise right, or left, lower leg forward.

7. Raise right, or left, lower leg backward.

8. Raise right, or left, lower leg sideward, right or left.

9. Circle right, or left, lower leg inward.

10. Circle right, or left, lower leg outward.

Complete command from *attention* would then be: 1. *Right lower leg,* 2. EXERCISE, 3. *Inward,* 4. CIRCLE, or, 3. *Forward,* 4. SWING, or, 3. *Sideward right,* 4. RAISE, 5. DOWN.

Fig. 50.

Continue, in all cases, by repeating the commands of execution. In the swings the leg is swung in the specified direction and at once returned to the starting position. In the raisings, the leg is held· in position until the command *down.*

FOOT AND TOES.

I. RAISING AND ROCKING.

1. Rise on toes. Fig. 51.
2. Rise on toes of right foot. Fig. 52.
3. Rise on toes of left foot.
4. Rise on toes and rock.
5. Rock from toes to heels.
6. Rise on heels. Fig. 53.
7. Rise on outer foot edge. Fig. 54.
Command: 1. *On toes,* 2. **RISE**, 3. **DOWN.**

Fig. 51.

Fig. 52.

In 1, 2, 3, the body is raised with life until the weight rests on the toes, heels together, knees straight; it is then lowered *gently* to the ground to avoid jarring.

Rocking on the toes is a series of short, springy extensions and bendings of the toe joints, the heels not being permitted to touch the ground. Rocking from toes to heels is executed by raising the body on the toes, then gently lowering the heels and raising the toes. In the rockings, continue by repeating *One, two.*

Fig. 53.

Fig. 54.

16200——3

II. BENDING AND CIRCLING.

1. Bend foot upward.   Fig. 55.
2. Bend foot downward.

Fig. 55.

3. Bend foot inward.   Fig. 56.

Fig. 56.

4. Bend foot outward.
5. Circle foot outward.
6. Circle foot inward.

The leg should first be raised to one of the positions (knee extended) described under: Leg—I. Raising, then command: 1. *Foot upward*, 2. **BEND**, 3. **BACK**.

The leg remains fully extended while the foot being is exercised.

In 5, 6, continue by repeating *One, two.*

STRADDLE POSITION.

This is a position where the feet are planted squarely on the ground, the distance from one to the other being equal to the length of the leg.

Fig. 57.

There are two kinds of straddle, side and cross.

To assume the former, command: 1. *Side straddle*, 2. **HOP**, 3. **RECOVER**. Fig. 57.

At the command *hop,* the knees are slightly bent and heels raised; then with a short, quick extension of the knees the body is forced upward and the legs separated. In alighting, the balls of the feet should strike the ground first, knees slightly bent and immediately afterward extended.

At the command *back,* leap upward and close the legs, alighting on the balls of the feet.

Fig. 58.

The cross straddle is similarly executed, it being necessary, of course, to indicate which leg is to be advanced, thus: 1. *Cross straddle, right forward,* 2. **HOP**, 3. **RECOVER**. Fig. 58.

The right leg is advanced and the left moved to the rear.

Fig. 59.

The position of side straddle may also be reached by twisting the legs, first inward on the balls of the feet, then planting the heels and twisting outward on the heels and planting toes, and so on until the proper distance is obtained. The command being: 1. *Side straddle*, 2. TWIST, 3. RECOVER. Fig. 59.

At command *back,* return to original position by twisting the legs first on heels, then on toes, and so on.

All of the arm, head, shoulder, trunk, and some of the leg and foot exercises can be executed while in this position.

LEANING REST.

POSITIONS.

It is not advisable to make beginners practice exercises while in this position. For advanced classes, however, they are highly recommended, since assuming the position itself brings into play nearly all the muscles of the trunk, arms, and legs. It may be reached in the following ways:

I.

Command: 1. *Knees full,* 2. BEND, 3. *Hands on floor* (between or on the outside of legs), 4. PLACE, 5. *To the leaning rest,* 6. TRAVEL, 7. RECOVER.

Execute *bend* and *place,* thus assuming a squatting position. At the command *travel,* move the hands forward, first the right then the left, until the body is fully extended. The body in this position should be perfectly rigid and rest on the toes and palms of hands; arms vertical, head up, and heels touching.

At the command *back,* move the hands backward, first the right then the left, and resume the squatting position. Continue by repeating *Travel, recover.*

II.

Command: 1. *Knees full,* 2. **BEND,** 3. *Hands on floor.* Fig. 60. 4. **PLACE,** 5. *Legs to the leaning rest.* Fig. 61. 6. **EXTEND,** 7. **RECOVER.**

At command *extend,* rest the weight of the body on the hands and extend the legs backward, assuming position.

At command *back,* resume squatting position, moving legs forward.

Continue by repeating *Extend, recover.*

Fig. 60.

III.

Command: 1. *Knees full,* 2. **BEND,** 3. *Hands on floor,* 4. **PLACE,** 5. *Arms forward to the leaning rest,* 6. **EXTEND,** 7. **RECOVER.**

At the command *extend,* the knees are extended, feet remaining in position, and the hands are thrown forward to the proper position.

At the command *recover,* the arms shove the body forcibly to the rear, the knees being bent at the same time, and the squatting position assumed.

Continue by repeating *Extend, back.*

Fig. 61.

IV.

Command: 1. *Trunk forward,* 2. **BEND,** 3. *To the leaning rest,* 4. **FALL,** 5. **RECOVER.**

At the command *bend,* the body is bent forward as far as possible, the hands being on or near the floor.

At the command *fall,* the body is slightly extended and permitted to fall forward on the hands, arms being bent as the hands strike, so as to break the force of the fall.

At command *recover,* assume the squatting position as in I, II, or III.

There are other ways of assuming the leaning rest, such as falling from an upright position, but, as there is more or less risk run in executing them, they have not been explained.

The general rule given under the head of **Commands,** concerning *halt,* should be borne in mind, as it determines when the position of the soldier is to be resumed in all cases.

EXERCISES.

While in the *leaning rest* position, the following exercises may be gone through with:

ARM.

Commands:

1. 1. *Right* (or *Left*) *arm forward,* 2. **RAISE,** 3. **DOWN.** Fig. 62.

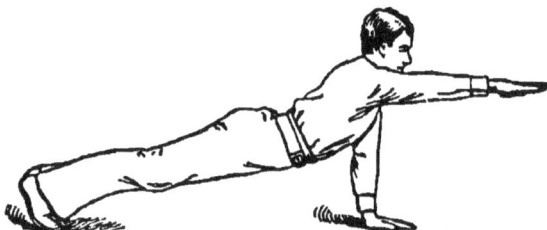

Fig. 62.

2. 1. *Right* (or *Left*) *arm sideward,* 2. **RAISE,** 3. **DOWN.**
3. 1. *Right* (or *Left*) *arm backward,* 2. **RAISE,** 3. **DOWN.**
4. 1. *Arms downward,* 2. **BEND,** 3. **BACK.** Fig. 63.

Fig 63.

5. 1. *Mark time with hands,* 2. ONE, 3. TWO.

At the command *one,* raise the left hand; at *two,* again ˀring back the left and raise the right, and so on.

6. 1. *Hop on hands,* 2. HOP.

7. 1. *Hop on and clap hands,* 2. HOP.

8. 1. *Right* (or *Left*) *arm forward* (or *backward*), 2. CIRCLE.

LEG.

Commands:

1. 1. *Right* (or *Left*) *leg backward,* 2. RAISE, 3. DOWN. Fig. 64.

2. 1. *Right* (or *Lett*) *leg sideward,* 2. RAISE, 3. DOWN.

3. 1. *Cross legs,* 2. CROSS, 3. BACK.   Fig. 65.

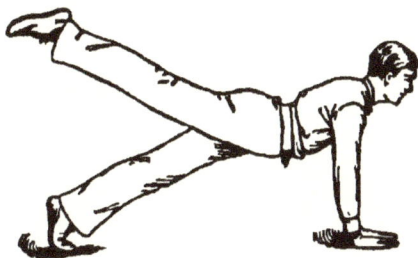 

Fig. 64.   Fig. 65.

4. 1. *Right* (or *Left*) *heel,* 2. RAISE, 3. DOWN.

5. 1. *Right* (or *Left*) *knee,* 2. RAISE, 3. DOWN.   Fig. 66.

Fig. 66.

6. 1. *Knees to squatting position,* 2. DRAW, 3. BACK.

7. 1. *Straddle legs,* 2. STRADDLE, 3. BACK.

8. 1. *Legs to straddle stand*, 2. DRAW, 3. BACK. Fig. 67.

Fig. 67.

9. 1. *Mark time with feet*, 2. ONE, 3. TWO (raise left first).
10. 1. *Hop on feet*, 2. HOP

ARM AND LEG.

Commands:

1. 1. *Right arm forward and left leg backward*, 2. RAISE, 3. DOWN. Fig. 68.

Fig. 68.

2. 1. *Left arm forward and right leg backward*, 2. RAISE, 3. DOWN.

3. 1. *Right arm and left leg sideward*, 2. RAISE, 3. DOWN.

4. 1. *Left arm and right leg sideward*, 2. RAISE, 3. DOWN.

5. 1. *Mark time with hands and feet*, 2. UP, 3. UP.

6. 1. *Hop on hands and feet*, 2. HOP.

7. 1. *Bend arms and straddle legs*, 2. BEND, 3. BACK. Fig. 69.

Fig. 69.

CIRCLING AND SQUATTING.

Commands:

1. 1. *Legs forward, right* (or *left*), 2. *To sitting position between hands*, 3. CIRCLE, 4. BACK.

At command *back,* resume original position by circling legs backward.

2. 1. *Forward to sitting position between hands,* 2. SQUAT, 3. BACKWARD, 4. SQUAT. Fig. 70.

At command *back,* resume original position by squatting or circling backward.

3. 1. *From forward to backward leaning rest,* 2. SQUAT, 3. BACK.

4. 1. *Legs from forward to backward leaning rest,* 2. CIRCLE, 3. BACK.

5. 1. *Complete circle with legs* (*right, left, or both*) *to the right* (or *left*), 2. CIRCLE.

Fig. 70.

SIDEWARD AND BACKWARD.

The position above described is known as the *forward leaning rest.* Being in this position, to assume the *sideward leaning rest,* the instructor commands:

1. *Sideward rest,* 2 *Right* (or *left*), 3. FACE.

At the command *face,* make a quarter turn with the body to the right; body resting on left hand, and ankle and outer edge of left foot; right arm in contact with right side; left side turned toward the ground.

Fig. 71.

To resume the *forward rest,* command: 1. *Forward rest,* 2. *Left* (or *right*), 3. FACE.

To assume *backward leaning rest,* the instructor commands: 1. *Backward rest,* 2. *Right* (or *left*) *about,* 3. FACE.

At the command *face*, make a half turn with the body to the right; body resting on both hands and both heels; arms vertical, hands to the front; back toward the ground, head up.

To resume the *forward rest*, command: 1. *Forward rest*, 2. *Right* (or *left*) *about*, 3. FACE. Fig. 72.

Fig. 72.

With a class of well-drilled men the backward rest may be assumed from the forward by circling the legs forward or by squatting forward between the hands. (See commands 3, 4, under *Circling and Squatting*.)

LUNGING.

Before executing the lunges, one of the direct or oblique-step positions should be assumed. Being in one of these, command: 1. LUNGE, 2. BACK. Fig. 73.

At the command *lunge* carry the foot that has been used in stepping about twice its length in the stepping direction and plant it fully and firmly, knee well bent, lower leg vertical; the other leg remains fully extended, foot flat on the ground.

At the command *back*, resume the stepping position.

The lunges may be combined with the various arm and trunk exercises.

Fig. 73.

For the sideward lunge, see Fig. 74.

Fig. 74.

GUARD POSITION.

In this position the right of the body is supported equally on both legs, knees slightly bent, feet nearly at right angles, firmly planted, twice the length of the foot apart, the one in rear 3 inches to the right or left of the one in front, one shoulder advanced the other thrown back, head erect, arms and hands in some one of the starting positions, preferably *hands on hips* or *arms to thrust*.

To assume the position, command:

1. 1. *Right* (or *Left*) *forward*, 2. GUARD, 3. RE-COVER. Fig. 75.

2. 1. *Right* (or *Left*) *sideward*, 2. GUARD, 3. RE-COVER.

3. 1. *Right* (or *Left*) *backward*, 2. GUARD, 3. RE-COVER.

4. 1. *In the various oblique directions*, 2. GUARD, 3. RECOVER.

Fig. 75.

In 1 at command *guard*, make a half face to the left, left toe pointing square to left, advance and place the right foot forward and assume above position.

In 2, 3, plant the right foot sideward or backward and assume above position, left toe pointing to the front.

GUARD STEP POSITION.

Commands:

1. 1. *Right* (or *Left*) *forward,* 2. **GUARD STEP,** 3. **RE-COVER.** Fig. 76.

2. 1. *Right* (or *Left*) *sideward,* 2. **GUARD STEP,** 3. **RE-COVER.** Fig. 77.

3. 1. *Right* (or *Left*) *backward,* 2. **GUARD STEP,** 3. **RE-COVER.** Fig. 78.

Fig. 76   Fig. 77.   Fig. 78.

4. 1. *Right* (or *Left*) *obliquely backward,* 2. **GUARD STEP,** 3. **RECOVER.**

5. 1. *Right* (or *Left*) *obliquely forward,* 2. **GUARD STEP,** 3. **RECOVER.**

The leg specified is moved forward much the same as in the *guard* position, but the knee is fully extended; knee of other leg is slightly bent and carries the weight of the body which is not turned, as in the *guard* position, but remains to the front. Arms as in latter.

HOPPING.

Hopping is executed by first raising the body on the balls of the feet, then springing from the ground by a series of short jumps. The knees remain easily extended, heels together and free from the floor. Arms having assumed some position, the instructor commands: 1. *On toes,* 2. **RISE**, 3. **HOP**.

At the command *hop,* make one spring alighting on the balls of the feet. Continue by repeating *One, two.* Of course, at the command *halt,* the exercise ceases.

HOPPING EXERCISES.

1. Hop and turn to the right or left at every second, fourth, or sixth hop.

2. Hop and turn about at every second, fourth, or sixth hop.

3. Hop to side straddle in four and return to attention in four hops.

4. Hop to side straddle and continue to hop in that position.

5. Hop to side straddle in one hop and return to attention in next hop.

6. Hop to cross straddle and return to attention in next hop.

7. Hop on right leg and hold left forward, sideward, or backward.

8. Hop on left leg and hold right forward, sideward, or backward.

9. Hop four times on right leg and then change and hop four times on left leg, holding the unemployed leg forward, sideward, or backward.

10. Same as 9, hopping twice on each leg.

11. Same as 9, hopping once on each leg.

12. Hop forward, sideward, or backward.

LEAPING.

Leaping or jumping as a calisthenic exercise has for its object the raising of the body from eight to twelve inches from the ground; there is no gaining of ground as in gymnastic jumping.

The instructor commands: 1. *Prepare to leap,* 2. **LEAP.**

At the first command, the arms are *raised forward* and the body elevated on the toes. At the command *leap,* the body is forced upward from the balls of the feet, by first slightly bending then quickly and forcibly extending the knees, the arms swinging forward shoulder high.

While the feet are off the floor, the legs remain extended and closed, the feet being closed but for a moment.

In alighting the balls of the feet touch the floor first, knees slightly bent; the latter are quickly extended, however, and the arms brought down by the sides.

Continue by repeating *leap.*

LEAPING EXERCISES.

1. Leap and execute a quarter of a turn to the right or left.

2. Leap and execute a half turn to the right or left.

3. Leap and straddle legs sideward (legs are closed) before alighting.

4. Leap and cross-straddle, right or left leg forward.

5. Leap and cross legs, right over left or left over right.

6. Leap and raise heels.

7. Leap and raise knees.

8. Leap and strike feet together.

9. Leap and strike feet together twice.

10. Leap and strike feet together three times.

11. Leap and cross and re-cross legs.

12. Leap and raise heels and touch them with hands.

13. Leap and swing arms sideward.

14. Leap and swing arms upward.

15. Leap and circle arms forward.
16. Leap and circle arms backward.
17. Leap and circle arms inward.
18. Leap and circle arms outward.
19. Leap and swing arms upward and execute a whole turn.

WALKING AND MARCHING.

The length of the full step in quick time is thirty inches, measured from heel to heel, and the cadence is at the rate of one hundred and twenty steps per minute.

The instructor having explained the principles and executed the step slowly, commands: 1. *Forward*, 2. **MARCH**. At the command *forward*, throw the weight of the body upon the right leg without bending the left knee. At the command *march*, advance and plant the left foot, which in turn supports the weight of the body while the right is being advanced and planted. The instructor indicates the cadence by calling one, two, three, four; or, left, right, the instant the left or right foot should be planted.

In executing the calisthenic exercises on the march the cadence should be at first given slowly and gradually increased as the men become more expert; some exercises require a slow and others a faster pace; it is best in these cases to allow the cadence of the exercise to determine the cadence of the step.

The men should march in a single rank at *proved intervals,* The command that causes and discontinues the execution should be given as the left foot strikes the ground.

On the march, to discontinue the exercises, command: 1. *Quick time*, 2. **MARCH**, instead of *Halt*, as when at rest.

All of the arm, wrist, finger, and shoulder exercises and some of the trunk and neck may be executed on the march by the same commands and means as when at rest.

The following leg and foot exercises are executed at the

command *march,* and the execution always begins with the left leg or foot.

1. 1. *On toes,* 2. MARCH.
2. 1. *On heels,* 2. MARCH.
3. 1. *On right heel and left toe,* 2. MARCH.
4. 1. *On left heel and right toe,* 2. MARCH.
5. 1. *On toes with knees stiff,* 2. MARCH.
6. 1. *Swing extended leg forward, ankle high,* 2. MARCH.
7. 1. *Swing extended leg forward, knee high,* 2. MARCH.
8. 1. *Swing extended leg forward, waist high,* 2. MARCH.
9. 1. *Swing extended leg forward, shoulder high,* 2. MARCH.
10. 1. *Raise heels,* 2. MARCH.
11. 1. *Raise knees,* 2. MARCH.
12. 1. *Raise knees, chest high,* 2. MARCH.
13. 1. *Circle extended leg forward, ankle high,* 2. MARCH.
14. 1. *Circle extended leg forward, knee high,* 2. MARCH.
15. 1. *Circle extended leg forward, waist high,* 2. MARCH.
16. 1. *Swing extended leg backward,* 2. MARCH.
17. 1. *Swing extended leg sideward,* 2. MARCH.
18. 1. *Raise knee and extend leg forward,* 2. MARCH.
19. 1. *Raise heels and extend leg forward,* 2. MARCH.

STEPS.

In the steps, the same rules as given above apply, viz: The command *march* given as the left foot strikes the ground, determines the execution which always begins with the left foot, and is kept up by each foot alternately until the command: 1. *Quick time,* 2. MARCH, when the direct step is resumed.

The different steps are executed by the following commands and means:

1. *Cross step,* 2. MARCH.

As the legs move forward they are crossed. The body does not turn.

1. *Halting step,* 2. MARCH.

The left foot is advanced and planted; the right foot is

brought directly to the rear of the left, resting on the ball only; the right is then advanced and planted and the left brought up, and so on.

1. *Foot-rocking step,* 2. **MARCH.**

The left foot is advanced and planted; the right foot is brought up beside it, heels touching; the body is then raised on the toes and lowered. The right foot is then advanced and planted and the left brought up, and so on.

1. *Change step,* 2. **MARCH.**

The left foot is advanced and planted; the toe of the right is then advanced near the heel of the left as in the *halting step;* the left foot is then advanced about half a step (15 inches) and the right steps off with the full step and is planted, the toe of the left foot being brought up, and so on.

1. *Knee-rocking step,* 2. **MARCH.**

A seach foot is planted it is accompanied by a slight bending and entension in the corresponding knee; the other leg remaining fully extended, heel raised.

1. *Lunging step,* 2. **MARCH.**

The length of the step is 45 inches, the knee in advance being well bent; the other leg remaining fully extended, heel raised.

1. *Leg balance step,* 2. **MARCH.**

The left foot is advanced, ankle high; it is then swung backward and forward and planted, the body during the swinging being balanced on the right leg. The right foot is then advanced, swung backward and forward and planted, and so on.

1. *Body balance step,* 2. **MARCH.**

The left foot is advanced, ankle high, body being bent slightly to the rear; the left foot is then swung backward, body being bent slightly to the front; the same foot is then swung forward again, and planted, the body in the meanwhile becoming erect. This is repeated with the right foot, and so on.

1. *Heel and toe step,* 2. **MARCH.**

16200——4

The left foot is advanced and allowed to rest on the heel; it is then swung backward and allowed to rest on the toes; it is once more advanced, and planted. This is repeated with the right foot, and so on.

1. *Cross step, raising knees,* 2. **MARCH.**

Execute the *cross step* and raise the knees. The cross step may also be executed in combination with the swings of the extended leg.

The *change step* may be combined with the following: *cross step, halting step, raising knees, foot-rocking step, on toes, raising heels, swinging and circling legs, heel and toe step.* These may also be combined with the *change step hop.*

1. *Change step hop,* 2. **MARCH.**

Execute the ordinary *change step,* hopping with the change.

1. *Forward gallop hop,* 2. **MARCH.**

The left foot is advanced and planted, the right is brought up in rear as in the *halting step;* this is done four times in succession. The same is done four times with the right foot in advance, and so on.

1. *Sideward gallop step,* 2. **MARCH.**

The left foot is advanced, body turning to the right: four hops are then executed sideward on the left foot followed by the right; at the fourth hop the body is turned to the left about and four hops executed sideward on the right foot followed by the left, and so on.

DOUBLE TIMING.

The length of the full step in double time is 36 inches; the cadence is at the rate of 180 steps per minute. To march in double time the instructor commands: 1. *Forward,* 2. *Double time,* 3. **MARCH.**

At the command *forward,* throw the weight of the body on the right leg; at the command *double time,* raise the hands until the forearms are horizontal, fingers closed, nails toward the body, elbows to the rear.

At the command *march,* carry the left foot forward, leg slightly bent, knee somewhat raised, and plant the foot 36 inches from the right; then execute the same motion with the right foot; continue this alternate movement of the feet, throwing the weight of the body forward and allowing a natural swinging motion to the arms. Head erect, shoulders back.

In the run, the cadence is faster than in the double time.

When marching in double time and in running, the men breathe as much as possible through the nose, keeping the mouth closed.

A few minutes at the beginning of the calisthenic exercises should be devoted to double timing. From lasting only a few minutes at the start it may be gradually in creased; so that daily drills should enable the men at the end of five or six months to double time for fifteen or twenty minutes without losing the breath or becoming fatigued.

After the double time the men should be marched for several minutes at quick time; after this the instructor should command: 1. *Route step,* 2. **MARCH.**

In marching at route step, the men are not required to preserve silence nor keep the step; if marching at proved intervals, the latter are preserved.

To resume the cadenced step in quick time, the instructor commands: 1. *Squad,* 2. **ATTENTION.**

Great care must be exercised concerning the duration of the double time and the speed and duration of the run.

The men should be cautioned to come down to quick time upon experiencing pain in the side.

When exercise rather than distance is desired, the running should be done on the balls of the feet, heels raised from the ground.

DOUBLE-TIMING EXERCISES.

While the men are double timing, the instructor may vary the position of the arms by commanding:

1. 1. *Arms forward,* 2. **RAISE.**
2. 1. *Arms sideward,* 2. **RAISE.**
3. 1. *Arms upward,* 2. **RAISE.**
4. 1. *Hands on hips,* 2. **PLACE.**
5. 1. *Hands on shoulders,* 2. **PLACE.**
6. 1. *Arms forward,* 2. **CROSS.**
7. 1. *Arms backward,* 2. **CROSS.**

At the command *down,* the double-time position for the arms and hands is resumed.

The instructor may combine the following with the *double time:*

1. 1. *Cross step,* 2. **MARCH.**
2. 1. *Raise knees,* 2. **MARCH.**
3. 1. *Raise heels,* 2. **MARCH.**
4. 1. *Swing legs forward,* 2. **MARCH.**
5. 1. *Swing legs backward,* 2. **MARCH.**

To discontinue these exercises, but still continue the double timing, command: 1. *Double time,* 2. **MARCH.** To march in quick time, command 1. *Quick time,* 2. **MARCH.** Marching in common, quick, or double time, to halt, command 1. *Squad,* 2. **HALT.**

INDEX.

O

www.ingramcontent.com/pod-product-compliance
Lightning Source LLC
Chambersburg PA
CBHW032046090426

42733CB00030B/710